A DAY AT THE BEACH

HOW ABSOLUTELY *ANYONE* CAN SUCCESSFULLY BUILD SAND CASTLES AND BUILD EVEN BETTER BEACH MEMORIES.

For Sue, my lovely wife and life-long beach friend.

She's the inspiration for this book.

A DAY AT THE BEACH

HOW ABSOLUTELY *ANYONE* CAN SUCCESSFULLY BUILD SAND CASTLES AND BUILD EVEN BETTER BEACH MEMORIES.

KEY SELECTIONS NARRATED
BY SAN D. SHOVEL

WRITTEN AND ILLUSTRATED BY D.R. SMITH
WITH THE EDUCATIONAL BEACH PRESS

Publishing Information

A Day at the Beach. How Absolutely Anyone Can Successfully Build Sand Castles and Build Even Better Beach Memories.

© 2003 Douglas R. Smith

Published by Educational Beach Press

121 Aspen Lane, Seven Fields PA 16046

Designed by Tom Kolarich, Mechanicsburg PA

Character "San D. Shovel" © 2003 Douglas R. Smith

Information about this book and Educational Beach Press is available through www.EducationalBeachPress.com or retail stores where this book can be purchased.

Library of Congress Information

Library of Congress Control Number: 2003113971

ISBN 0-9743967-0-2

PREFACE

The sub title of A Day at the Beach is *How Absolutely Anyone Can Successfully Build Sand Castles and Build Even Better Beach Memories.* How do these blend together -- the beach, playing in the sand and finding memorable enjoyment? Hopefully, an answer will become very clear with even the most quick, cursory skim through this book.

Here's the basic concept: Sand castles and sand sculptures have a magical aura. But, unfortunately, that same aura sometimes seems not totally welcoming to those who are at the beach for only a Saturday afternoon or on a week's vacation time. All too often, sand sculpting seems beyond our capabilities, off limits or just an unnecessary expenditure of time.

Thus, a major objective of this book is to show that sand castles and sand sculptures are actually very, very easy to build. Complementing the simplicity of sand castles, we ought to recognize the extraordinary opportunity of sharing sand play with people we like and people we love. A few hours of creativity -- whether packing sand to create a sea turtle or learning to gently carve a castle turret -- are hours when we can be side-by-side with our parents, our children, our grandchildren, our family and our friends.

Get a one-use camera. Take a picture of the group around the sand castle. Frame the resulting photo as an 8 X 10: Three generations, sitting around a partially carved sand castle, our feet in the castle moat. Shoulder to shoulder, hunched into our work, we squint into the details of our structure. As we carve, we chat. As we chat, we learn even more about one another than we already knew. We share. We enjoy one another. We build sand castles. We build the best of memories.

-- DRSmith

WHERE TO FIND STUFF

Beach Tips from San D. Shovel show up randomly throughout A Day at the Beach.

I. INTRODUCTION TO A DAY AT THE BEACH

Low-slung beach chairs provide us a perfect perspective to absorb our surroundings and quietly layer in the images that will become our memories.

From this comfortable point of view, we can slowly soak in the visual images around us while focusing on people -- those we're with and those about whom we care the most. This day is devoted to us. It's dedicated to our being near one another, talking, chatting, joking, chuckling, laughing. Our chatter even may evolve into some reasonably serious conversations about our lives and world events. That's okay. In fact, it's even good. Our time is generally pretty limited during the day-to-day hum of life, so this day at the beach is a good way to share what we might not otherwise share. Let's think of this time and being here together as somewhat akin to the old time television shows in which families had time for long dinner-table conversations.

We should prime our environment so our activities and quiet times are enjoyable. But we don't need to do all that much. The beach environment is naturally conducive with memorable happiness.

Let's consider where we are. In a beach chair. Our eyes are droopy, near closed. If we gently drop one hand over the arm of the chair, we feel the surface and texture of the warm sand. A slow side-to-side sweeping motion moves the sand and forms a fan-like furrow. It feels nice.

The sun and its warmth have drawn us to this spot. A bad day is still a good day for the beach. On a good day, the warm sun is soothing and assuring. On a perfect day, the sun and the soft breeze complement one another to simultaneously toast and cool the skin.

Thinking back a bit to the ride here, it was our noses, not our eyes that gave the first indication we were approaching the ocean. Recall a sweet salty smell that sneaked in with us for the final 10 or 20 minutes of our trip. Once at the beach, our olfactory sense finds diversions elsewhere, making the salty fragrance difficult to detect. Still, our nostrils join in with our shoreline celebration, detecting even the warmth of the air and the sand. More fragrances -- sunscreens, sun blocks, oils and creams. Pool chlorine. Tropical smells of coconut and pineapple.

Taste sensations also play a role in this process of creating truly memorable images. The simple taste of ice tea. Diet cola diluted by melted ice. Creamy, tropical smoothies. Fresh pineapple, cantaloupe and grapes. Do we risk boardwalk fries at the water's edge, where seagulls have perfected the art of pecking fries from unprotected cups? After all, we can only find those fries here! Maybe later during an evening walk. Or maybe much later, after working through an all-you-can-eat order with steamed crabs, bay seasoning and cole claw. For now, it's cold ice water through a straw, with a hint of lemon.

The sounds are unique. The sounds can be duplicated only in our heads. Not electronically or digitally -- at least not in a manner that evokes what we really feel at the beach. The sounds are the beach. A fluttering umbrella. Rustling palm leaves. Nearby muffled conversations. Chattering children and the occasional shriek. Back, behind us there may be sounds of building construction. But, after all, who doesn't want to be here? A distant radio. The far-off steel drums from the shaded beach-hut tribute band singing Jimmy Buffett's "…made enough money to buy Miami…" But the compelling and most memorable constant sound is the water. It's the waves toppling into the sand. Over and over. Steady. Lightly rolling and pounding or heavily rumbling and crashing. It's always the water.

Now, look around. Let's really take it in. What will our minds capture that's outside the range and sensitivity of a good disposable panoramic camera?

The horizon pulls at our vision. It's that flat line where the water is darker than the sky and distant thunderheads offer their own stark white contrast to both. The pale sand is evenly dimpled by millions of footsteps. The same sand reflects its warmth and treats us to viewing everything through a wavy shimmering light. Where else but the beach does the word "shimmering" actually have meaning? Here, the bright of colors are always brighter and catch our eye.

We note the striped beach umbrellas. The colorful beach tents. The clusters of color in a circle of beach blankets. People in bathing suits. Beautiful people. Regular people. A full spectrum of people. "Pale invaders and tanned crusaders," as Mr. Buffett might say. Each of us is equally welcomed and comfortably correct on our brightly colored blankets, on our towels, in our lounges and in our low slung beach chairs.

Narrowing our focus to nearby, here are the people we care about most. They are why we are here at the beach, so we can all share this moment, share the warmth of the sun, share this experience and share this day.

Our hand slowly strokes the sand, back and forth, uncovering tiny shoreline shells and glistening gems. This is a day for savoring sensations and building memories. This is a day at the beach.

Unforgettable beach memories

BUILDING BETTER BEACH MEMORIES

If this were a traditional book, it would build to a climax -- the dénouement, grand finale. Then it would end, and we'd look for new reading material. In a traditional sequence, we would describe our understanding of memories and sand sculpture construction in the culminating chapters coming only on the heels of the preparatory information that better equips us to grasp the full, intense meaning of sand play.

But because this isn't a traditional book, we're going to collect the memories first. After that, we'll explore sculpting a good sand castle. Most publishers prefer their books have an identifiable beginning, middle and end. Fact is, *A Day at the Beach* could be skimmed backwards, read by turning to every other page or simply thumbing to stop at pictures. Regardless of where we land, we ought to find help and entertainment.

II. GATHERING MEMORIES

There are dozens of ways we can gather and store our beach memories -- scrap books, videos, photo albums, jars of shells, jars of sand, personally appealing art work and other unique collectible items. In the end, nothing will ever provide safe harbor for

our memories quite as well as a solo photograph hanging framed on the family room wall, sitting on the bedside stand or stuck to the refrigerator door. It can be an 11 X 14 or a small snap shot. Whether it's a beautiful red sunset or a family posing in front of a beach house, it's the vacation photo that most easily and most quickly returns us to a mindset of pleasure, comfort and happiness. All it takes is one glance at that photo.

If there's one post-vacation tradition we need to establish, it's selecting our favorite photo or photos, getting frames and putting them all in visible locations where those 8 X 10's make us smile each and every time we pass. This step is more important than tossing the suitcases into a back closet. This act -- saving and framing our favorite photos -- will last the rest of our lives.

Invigorating our Memories

There's an interesting approach for strengthening our mental faculties to invigorate our memories. The concept is an easy one and takes almost no time or training to master. It magnifies our abilities to more vividly recall events, surrounding and circumstances.

This approach is to take a few moments to "five sense" our surroundings. In other words, for us to soak in an entire enjoyable situation, we will want to fill every available memory cell with every aspect of this moment. We do it by calling on all five of our senses to absorb all possible sensations.

See more. Typically, we will recall visuals around us. But we can further magnify our visual memory by looking around and consciously taking in a broader view than we might otherwise do.

Hear more. Most of us will recall the sounds of a memorable occasion, whether they're voices, laughter, rustling leaves, the pounding surf, a certain song or the weather-related sounds of wind or rain. But, as with vision, we can further amplify our memory's link to pleasurable events and moments by taking an extra second to intently listen to what our ears are picking up around us. For those of us with more literal audio preferences, a favorite purchase is the ocean sound of a conch shell.

Beyond photography, great beach memories can be saved in jars, boxes and tins for rediscovery later on.

Focusing closely on items, such as the texture of a rain-drenched sand castle, is another way of capturing memories.

BEACH TIP:

WHEN IT COMES
TO BEACH MEMORIES,
DERMATOLOGISTS WARN
US OUR SCALP ISN'T AS
DURABLE AS THE SKIN ON
SHOULDERS, ARMS AND
LEGS. BETTER TO WARMLY
RECALL THE FRAGRANCE
AND FEEL OF SUN BLOCK
THAN KNOW THE SEARING
PAIN OF SUN BURN.

Breath deeply to smell more. We all have unique memories based on smells and fragrances, both pleasant and unpleasant. Some of our best memories can be from a county fair and cow barn. Unpleasant odors and joyful recollections. A beach has its own smells -- salt, warm sand, sun screen, fish, some more pleasant than others -- and we need to learn to draw in and record those fragrances deep within our memory, where they become part of the overall comfort and happiness of the day.

Taste more. We may not be quick to connect taste with our beach experience. Most of our time at the beach is not spent eating food, but our meals are typically times when groups of friends and family gather. It's a time we'll want to vividly remember. What we do eat can contribute significantly to our potentially positive memories, if we'll take the extra second to mentally link our food with our immediate surroundings. Cotton candy with board walks. Ice cream and people watching. Lobster, butter and tasting the salt air. Thick, sweet drinks with warm air and cool shade from an umbrella.

Touch to feel more. We tend to forget about the memories from touch, and they can be imbedded just as easily and intensely as any visual or audio thought. We merely need to focus on touch and what we feel for those times we want to vividly recall. Think about the sand: Is the sand too hot? Warm? Cool? Wet? Dry? Full of stones or shells? Coarse? Soft? Powdery? This is once sensation that is nicely rekindled if we scoop up a small amount of sand and save it in a jar. Later, back home, we have our beach in a jar to see, smell and feel.

Photographic memories are most common because they portray the moment at hand -- children at play, posed groups or quiet settings.

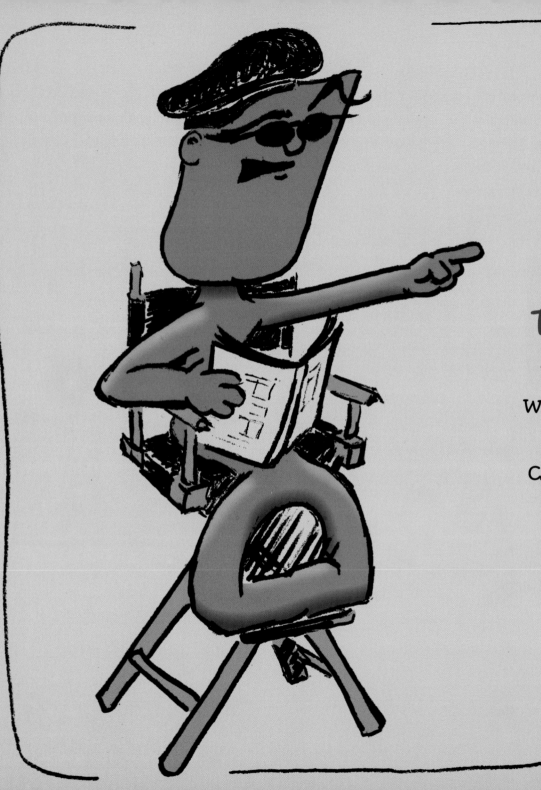

GREAT ROLES IN SAND SCULPTING: THE DIRECTOR.

WE SHOULD SELECT SOMEONE WHO PROVIDES LEADERSHIP AND PERSPECTIVE FOR OUR SAND CASTLE PROJECT. CAUTION: THIS ROLE CAN BE POLITICIZED IF OUR GROUP ISN'T CAREFUL.

All senses. Ultimately, our most fond memories will be the interaction with those we care about -- our family, old friends, newly discovered friends. With them we want to forever recall our conversations, our jokes, our shared laughter and our experiences. To completely grab and hold on to those people, events and surroundings that we so richly cherish, we need allow our minds to capture every aspect of each occasion. All five senses can record the processes. All we need to do is think about our surroundings for a few split seconds and hit our mental "record button." Our senses and mind will do the rest.

Sand sculpting has its own healthy and valuable competition with beach attractions such as volleyball, snorkeling, shelling, walking, sailing, site-seeing or just plain lounging.

Artwork like sketches, paintings and sculptures can remain as constant reminders of our shared time together.

We collect memories
through all sensations: sight,
smell, hearing, touch and taste.

III. OUR SPOT IN THE SAND

No matter how hard we try to be organized, our walk onto the beach and toward the water looks like a nomadic caravan scene from Lawrence of Arabia. We tote beach blankets, towels, coolers, chairs and toys. We carry umbrellas, tents, beach bags and beach books. We drag strollers whose wheels are entirely unsuited to sand.

But this is where the great memories begin, and by evening we'll laugh about slogging through those final 20 yards of sand.

Our spot in the sand is important to us. It's our encampment. It's where our family, friends and clan will claim its turf for anywhere from a few hours to two weeks. Once we've staked out our claim in this ocean-front frontier, no other homesteaders can drag their household goods and furniture into our circle of wagons, umbrellas, chairs and blankets.

It seems some portions of sand turf are extraordinarily desirable. If we get up early to watch, just as the sun is rising with its pink-gray-dawn glow, we'll see small bands of vacationers, dragging chairs stealth-like onto the beach to claim key strategic locations. They deliberately overload themselves with paraphernalia that gets used to stake out the widest possible plots of turf. They are able to anticipate beach-based market demands and prepare their site against the inevitable hoards of arriving inland day-trippers.

Sometimes we need to smile at our own quirkiness.

Finding our Spot

Arriving for our first day, we drag our beach gear through throngs
of people as we search for an opening in the landscape. We slow
our pace and eye a potential site of our own. We've avoided the
tracts marked by empty chairs covered with neatly folded, unused
towels and unopened paperback books. We've also avoided
what looks to be an encampment of Civil War reconstructionists
equipped with chairs, umbrellas, canopies, tents and coolers the
size of horse trailers.

It's been a tough trek, but now we see between us and the water's edge another group of notorious sand turf defenders -- The Professional Sun Worshippers -- very darkly tanned people who have already been at the beach for a full week of vacation. With every possible signal, they tell us they are veterans and they have been here much longer than we have. They have well-established preening poses. They stand, stretch and turn to demonstrate their full tanning. They tug at bathing suits so it looks as though they're improving their comfort, when their true goal is to demonstrate their distinct, well-established tan lines. They pull off caps to unveil sun-bleached hair. And the clincher -- they toss to a fellow Sun Worshipper a bottle of Hawaiian Tropic Dark Tan SPF 4. With every movement, they scream "Our beach. Forever!"

We turn our caravan a bit to the north, shuffle in our own small circle and drop our bundles. Finally, we have located our spot in the sand.

Oftentimes a quiet walk on to the beach leads us into a mass of beach humanity.

Boardwalk, cliff side or state park doesn't really matter so long as we have access to a sandy beach where we can walk on along the water's edge, sit on a blanket or stand and gaze at a sunset.

Understanding High Tide

Here's a hint for the making this a better day. Check with the Weather Channel on TV, with weather.com or in the local resort newspaper to learn when tides are coming in and going out. Key is knowing what time high tide hits and figure out where it will reach on the beach.

To the water side of the tide line is the smooth, water-flattened sand. To the upper side of the tide line is the trampled, noticeably disturbed sand that is untouched by recent waves. Another clue may be small shells and debris pushed by waves to create a visible high-tide line.

No one wants soaked beach blankets, so let's check the times for high tide and figure out how high it will reach on the beach.

Selecting an Ideal Spot for Sand Play

Positioning is among the keys to successful sand sculpting. We want to be near enough to the water's edge that we have quick access for carrying and dumping water to moisten our pile of pre-construction sand. Still, we can't be too close to the tumbling waves, because high tide could prematurely wipe out our work and guarantee we're among the beach-goers with dripping wet blankets.

Perhaps the ideal sand castle site is at the high tide line -- the line that shows us where waves rolled to a stop during high tide. If we build just at the high-tide line, we can create an adjacent base camp next to or around our construction site. We and our colleagues can easily roam within a 15 to 20 foot area to keep our refreshments and nourishment, while remaining close to the job.

The ideal setting is basically a plot where we can all gather and be within normal talking range of one another.

If waterfront property is all taken, we can set up our site back from the water and recruit water bearers to soak our sand. Or we can dig an extremely deep hole to pull out moist sand from below the surface.

The water's edge shifts with the tides and while it's helpful to be close to water for wetting our sand sculpting area, we need to be careful we're not so close to the edge that high tide creeps in and rolls over our work.

Sand Moisture

There are a few simple rules regarding the physical properties of mixing sand and water to create the best of sand sculpting environments, let's keep it simple.

- Dry sand is useless. It won't work. It cannot be shaped into anything beyond cone-shaped mounds.

- Soaking wet sand can be used to create an interesting "drizzle" technique in sand sculpting but is somewhat difficult to manage.

"Beach front property" is valuable and typically crowded and chaotic. At times, it seems as though it's wall-to-wall blankets, towels and bodies. Still, we can find a way to squeeze in a sand castle, perhaps by recruiting from a neighboring umbrella.

- Moist sand works best for the widest array of sand sculpting projects. This can be accomplished by pouring water on to a pile of sand and letting it settle into and through the sand naturally.

How do we create just the right level of moisture in sand? The answer is to allow the sand to do it for us. The easiest way is to build a pile of sand and continually pour water on it. As we mound the pile higher, we add water. Shovel on four inches of sand; pour on water. Shovel on four more inches. More water.

The sand accepts the right amount of moisture and drains away unneeded water.

In other words, we want the moisture to be a reasonable balance that allows us some carving, patting, smoothing and shaping. And the sand seems to understand our preferences.

Once we carve and the sand is actually drying, we need to avoid touching it again. A close up look tells us that a crust-like surface is being baked by the sun and warmth. This phenomenon will keep our details in place for hours and hours, perhaps even all night. But it'll crumble if we try to reshape it.

Sand Shapes and Molds

Commercial plastic sand shapes and molds provide excellent detail for our uniquely memorable projects. As with moisture content in carving and shaping, our sand molds work best with an even balance of moisture. Too dry, the sand won't hold. Too wet, the sand will become partially stuck inside the mold, leaving us with a slightly mutilated castle tower.

With experience, we'll learn that the inside walls of our molds need to be pretty dry. We may be able to create only two or three near-perfectly detailed castle elements before an individual mold needs to be set aside to dry. This calls for our keeping a couple of molds on hand or shifting to shovel work, if our favorite molds become too wet.

A tall sand pile near the high-tide line is a near-perfect placement for sand castles, because it allows for easy access to water and increases the likelihood of a steep sand incline that makes ocean-side carving easier and adds an aesthetic impact finishing a castle that appears to tower over the landscape and water.

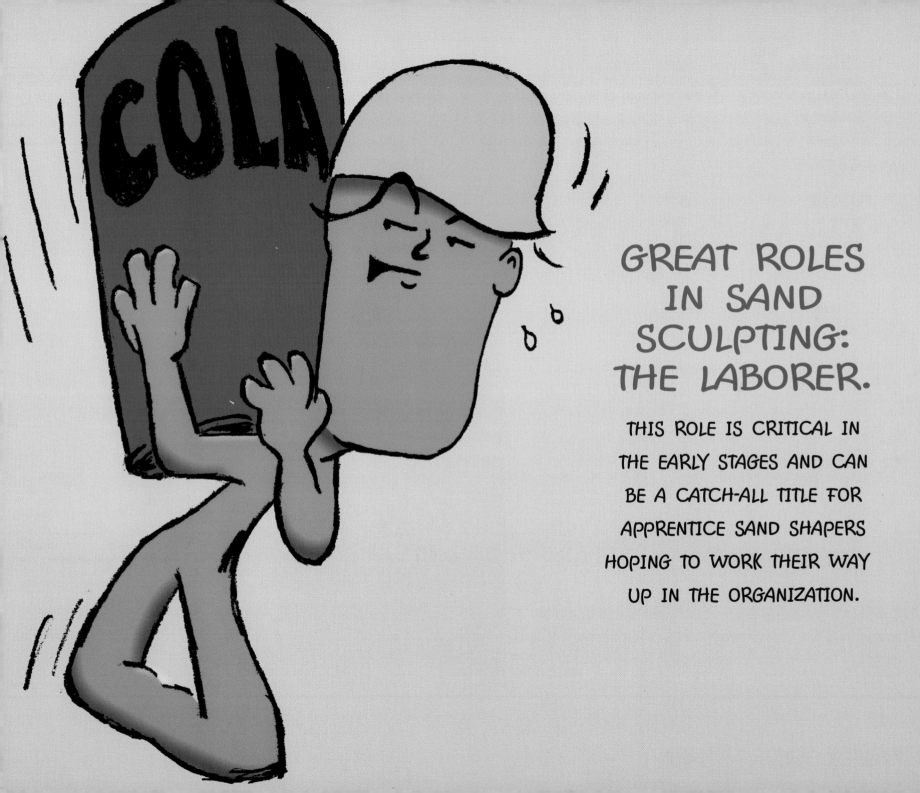

GREAT ROLES
IN SAND
SCULPTING:
THE LABORER.

THIS ROLE IS CRITICAL IN
THE EARLY STAGES AND CAN
BE A CATCH-ALL TITLE FOR
APPRENTICE SAND SHAPERS
HOPING TO WORK THEIR WAY
UP IN THE ORGANIZATION.

Top-down work always works best because of the drying sand. Once carved or shaped at the top of our mound, that sand will dry and form its crust while we uncover fresh, moist sand by cutting down into it.

One of the advantages to group projects is our sharing of experiences as we work with the sand. There will always be a certain amount of trial and error and personal styles that work better than other styles. We can benefit by observing and tutoring one another.

- Fine sand allows us to create extremely precise details with small tools and molds. But when fine sand dries, some of those details may disappear with the gentlest of breezes.

- Coarse sand allows us to work with larger scale to create large, thick walls befitting a toy action figure or create oversized sea creatures. Coarse sand also can restrict our use of sand castle molds and can be a bit harsh on hands. Better to use tools to scoop on coarse sand.

Differences in Sand

For the most part, we can sculpt and shape any type of sand we encounter. However, while we can create very interesting sculptures with any type of sand, different types do offer unique problems and opportunities. Here are the two extremes:

Ideal sand sculpting is on a near-perfect day with near-perfect sand . But there's no question that less-than-perfect days can nicely result in satisfying sand castle construction.

Most of us will encounter sand that combines the characteristics of both styles.

The Gulf Coast of Florida offers the full spectrum of sand styles from fine to coarse and everywhere in between. We can find every sand sample -- from the absolutely beautiful beaches of Destin and the Panhandle, where our feet disappear into soft white powder, to the gorgeous reflective sparkling sand of Naples, where we can gather shells of all sizes almost everywhere on the beach and protect the bottoms of our feet with sand footies or flip flops.

We can thoroughly enjoy sand sculpting, but we won't build the same two sand castles at these two differ types of beach.

These extremes help define our uniquely valuable memories. Each beach provides us with its own version of vacations that might otherwise be the same. At the Outer Banks, we may design our sand structure to accommodate a narrower section of a somewhat steep sloping incline. At Geneva-on-the-Lake, Ohio, we'll plan on building walls around our sandcastle, using the four-inch smooth, flat stones we find in the sand.

High tide can be a blessing or a curse, depending on our preference for sand castle longevity. We can enjoy the process either way -- whether our castle topples or withstands the approaching tide.

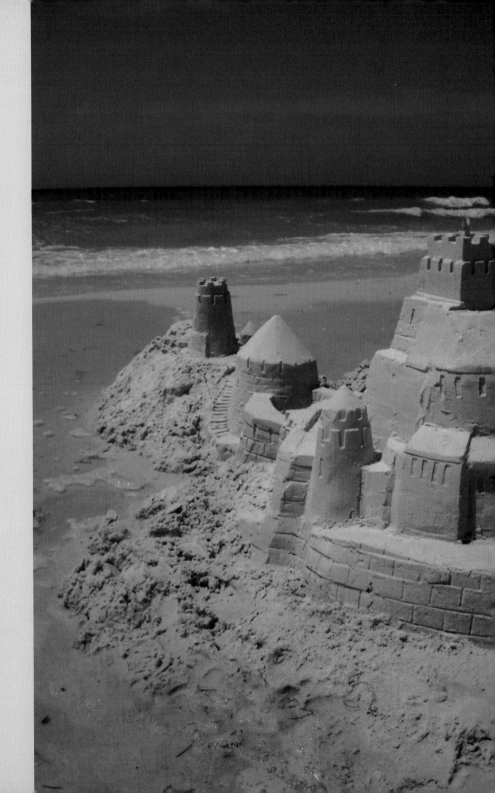

IV. BEACHES AND SHORELINES

We locate beaches where ever we can. We're hoping to play in the sand, hear the water and feel the warmth. One in five of us in will travel to a shoreline each summer for a day, a week or more if we can. We're drawn to oceans, gulfs, bays and lakes -- some place we can walk through soft sand to reach water, where we'll wade out far enough to get our rolled-up pants just a little wet.

More than half of the US states have shorelines with various types of rocks, marsh, silt or sand -- 29 states where people can throw down a towel on a sandy beach to enjoy the sun.

For those of us with no immediate access to a natural beach, we learned as children that we can always find a sandbox. We all have them near by -- in parks, playgrounds and often in our own backyards. We can use sandboxes as our fall-back beaches, especially if a pool is near by. After all, for most of us, sandbox's are where we first learned to love sand play.

Interestingly, our own myopia may limit our exposure to the variety and the vast number of beaches available to us. We seem like Canadian Geese with a pond, in that we generally find a beach we

enjoy and return there year after years. Of course, limited time, ease of travel or budgets may also narrow our scope of beach excursions. To that point, the best beach is the beach we're at!

With so many water fronts and beaches throughout the US, western hemisphere or the world, it's no wonder our beaches all differ. For example, a Floridian jogging along the winding pavement of Miami's South Beach wouldn't necessarily view Erie, Pennsylvania's Presque Isle as a vacation beach. Indeed, the jogger might conclude that South Beach "has it all over" Presque Isle, because South Beach really does have a beautifully long 12-month summer. Give us the choice between an all-expenses paid vacation to South Beach or Presque Isle, most of us will take South Beach.

Yet, Presque Isle has everything we need for a beautiful day at the beach -- miles of sand, warm sun, rolling waves, panoramic views and people who are with us to enjoy the day.

While there are advantages to the hundreds of resort communities along the US and nearby island coastlines, we are all within fairly quick striking distance of a great beach. Whether taking a lunch break on the beach in downtown Chicago, drinking coffee and reading the Sunday LA Times in the sand below Santa Monica Blvd or lining up 10 weekend trips to a rented house on the Jersey Shore, we compress our beach time into mini or extended vacations. We cherish the time. We cherish the memories.

We all find ways to thoroughly enjoy the beach we've found.

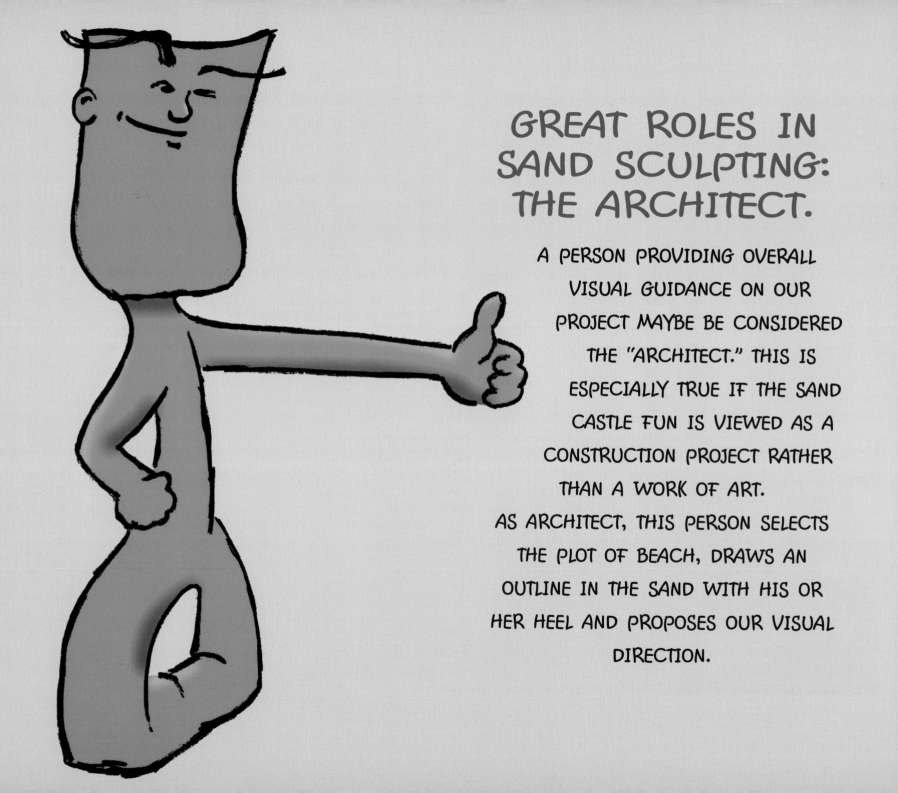

GREAT ROLES IN SAND SCULPTING: THE ARCHITECT.

A PERSON PROVIDING OVERALL VISUAL GUIDANCE ON OUR PROJECT MAYBE BE CONSIDERED THE "ARCHITECT." THIS IS ESPECIALLY TRUE IF THE SAND CASTLE FUN IS VIEWED AS A CONSTRUCTION PROJECT RATHER THAN A WORK OF ART.

AS ARCHITECT, THIS PERSON SELECTS THE PLOT OF BEACH, DRAWS AN OUTLINE IN THE SAND WITH HIS OR HER HEEL AND PROPOSES OUR VISUAL DIRECTION.

Beaches and Organized Sand Play

One hint as to what we do as a quiet diversion at the beach would be to observe or join in with the competition at one or more of the 40 annual sand sculpting contests held in the Western Hemisphere.

Sand sculpting competitions draw an active but relatively small number of people into a specific, unique facet of beach life. For most of us who favor walks along the water's edge, soaking in the surroundings and just maybe building a small castle, these contests can be excellent venues to observe and learn the sand-sculpting techniques from people who are extremely good at their craft. Although the sculpting is generally intimidating because it's just so good, it is, after all, just sand and water.

If we view sculpting as the art and sand as the artist's medium, we need to recall that sand is a beautifully forgiving medium. If sand slides and crumbles, we repair it. Easy. So after learning through contest observations, we could arrive at the conclusion that -- along with a few friends and family members -- we could return next year to enter and compete.

As with the differing locales -- from Washington State to Washington DC's "summer capital" in Rehoboth Beach, Delaware -- we're going to find differing types of beaches and differing textures of sand, which will influence our sculpting or castle building.

Beaches differ only in their geographic location. Once there, we gain the same levels of soothing relaxation or stimulating excitement.

It's also fascinating that sand sculpting competitions are not limited to sunny beaches wrapped with warm breezes and the sound of crashing waves in the background. Not at all. We'll find sand castle contests in Colorado, Idaho and Nebraska. A Fort Lauderdale organization builds magnificent sand sculptures in any setting from beaches to indoor malls.

Beaches differ vastly but lure us consistently

Most beach communities will provide contest details through a website. Also, a Texas-based, beach organization calling itself Sons of the Beach® maintains an on-line calendar of sculpting contests scheduled throughout the world at www.sandcastlecentral.com.

Beaches and shorelines differ in their sand and general terrain. Some beaches may have fine, soft sand, and other regions have a more coarse and rocky sand. Either is extremely enjoyable and provides excellent raw materials for sand castle construction.

Some of the U.S. Beaches Hosting Sand Castle Contests

- California --Arcata, Cannon Beach, Corona Del Mar, Crown Beach, Drakes Beach, Imperial Beach, Seal Beach, Ventura
- Connecticut -- Bridgeport
- Colorado -- Great Sand Dunes National Monument
- Delaware -- Rehoboth Beach
- Florida -- Clearwater Beach, Ft. Lauderdale, Ft. Myers Beach, Miami Beach, Pensacola Beach
- Idaho -- Sandpoint
- Maryland -- Ocean City
- Massachusetts -- Crane Beach
- Nebraska -- Lake McConaughy
- New Hampshire -- Hampton Beach
- New Jersey -- Asbury Park, Belmar and Fairlawn
- New York -- Amagansett Bay
- Oregon -- Portland
- Texas -- Corpus Cristi, Galveston, Port Aransas, South Padre Island
- Virginia -- Virginia Beach
- Washington -- Long Beach, Ocean Shores, Pacific Beach

Go to www.sandcastlecentral.com for a current list.

A tribute to sand castles highlights a walk along the board walk of Virginia Beach.

Cleanest Beaches

Each year the Clean Beaches Council announces its Blue Wave designation to apprise consumers of those beaches that are evaluated as clean and healthy -- and not significantly affected by litter. Annual details are at www.cleanbeaches.org.

As the sun slides down behind the horizon, there's a calm that drifts across the beach, letting us know to pause and remember another really good day at the beach.

PLAYING IN THE SAND

A lmost anything can serve as a tool for sand sculpting and sand castle construction. As a guide and following a bit of common-sense logic, small endeavors with the sand generally require smaller tools. Larger efforts that start with enormous piles of sand will require somewhat larger tools and -- assuming we don't have a backhoe parked at the dune line -- we'd be real smart to have a long handled shovel or two so we can create a basic pile of sand at our construction site.

V. OUR SAND TOOLS

Let's start small. With a toddler under an umbrella or sun tent we can work quite nicely with a plastic sand shovel, a few sand molds and a pail. Larger groups of adults, teens and youngsters can be a bit more resourceful in terms of searching out commonplace items to serve as sand shovels, scoops and tools.

Cup Collection. All we need are a few paper and plastic cups and maybe a plastic deli bowl. Add in a flat stick, and we're underway with our sand castle sculpting.

If there's no boardwalk or souvenir shop handy for buying a basic set of sand molds, let's consider some every day alternatives:

- **Plastic beverage cups** -- any size works but larger sizes would be better.

- **Paper cups** are okay for the short term but don't last long once they get wet.

- **Plastic eating utensils** are useful for carving in the sand -- drawing trenches or notching walls.

- **A well-used paperback book** can also serve out its final days as a plowing device or wall smoother.

- **A scrub bucket** from the hotel or house digs great holes and looks like a castle turret.

- **Windshield scrapers** (for snowbirds or others with snow experience) has several flat surfaces that can be used in sand carving.

- **Also from the car,** look for any items with edges that can be used in working or smoothing the sand -- such as laminated maps, cardboard nail files, small plastic storage boxes.

- **A flat stick** -- about the size of a paint stirrer -- is perhaps one of the most versatile sand tools available and can usually be found near beach dunes where now-broken sticks had served as slats for erosion and hurricane fences. If we have no other beach tools or toys, we could create a sand sculpture with just a pile of sand and a flat stick.

Great winding stairways can be notched from the top and working downward by gently carving, tapping and packing with the plastic shovel handle.

Bigger Stuff

Any group of energetic people gathered together for a day at the beach can become an eager labor pool for mounding up a good-sized pile of sand. Once that's done, we can create anything we want to create.

Realistically, we need digging tools that are suited for our tasks but also matched with our individual, physical capabilities and limitations.

Long-handle shovels are best for not straining backs. So, those among us with somewhat weaker, perhaps less developed or formerly injured lower back muscles, should grab the long-handled shovels. Long-handle spades are pretty abundant in the garage at home and for beach trips can be kept in a car or truck.

Flat-face shovels are handy later on for preliminary sand carving and shaping -- regardless of handle length. The idea beach shovel is less commonplace but would have a long-handle and flat-face. Less back strain and more preliminary, flat-edge sand carving.

Buckets, pails and bowls have multiple uses. For scooping sand to create our big sand pile, there are any number of available cleaning buckets, toy pails, five-gallon plastic buckets and bowls. In addition to their digging duties, they may also serve as water containers and superb cylindrical or dome-shaped sand molds. Plastic kitchen bowls come in an unlimited range of shapes and sizes.

An advantage to using buckets and pails is that they can be sized according to each person's individual capability for carrying sand and water. As a serious warning, these tools can lead to lower back strain, if we're not cautious and patient.

Gardening hand tools can be handy at the beach, especially the little spades, shovels, trowels and rakes we use for planting flowers and herbs. If there are a few in the garage or shed, we can toss them in for the trip and be ready to dig, cut and carve the sand immediately after we've spread our blankets and opened our beach chairs. A caution on garden tools: plastic's safer than

metal at the beach, because plastic doesn't get as hot in the sun or wound skin as easily as metal. Also, be sure to leave multi-pronged, sharp-tipped rakes in the garage or shed.

Kitchen utensils are only of serious value for digging deep holes in the sand if you're under the age of two and think "deep" is a six-inch hole. However, kitchen utensils are excellent sand-carv-ing tools. We can select from any number available in a kitchen drawer -- and the best include butter knives, tea spoons, soup or stirring spoons, flat-faced spatulas, smooth-edged cake and pie cut-ters, smaller plastic bowls, wooden crab mallets, plastic rolling pins and almost anything pointy or smooth.

Wooden mallets are among our tools. Take a close look at this sculptor's hands. Those are mallets for cracking hard shell crabs.

A bucket can scoop the sand and be an artistic turret.

Creating Crisp Details

Sand molds and tools are usually at a nearby beach shop. These are the creative items uniquely designed for sand and beach use. Sand molds and tools can produce absolutely fantastic results. Smooth. Detailed. Identifiable images. These things are just neat. We can easily imagine King Arthur watching the invading Celts from his tower wall -- whether or not it's historically accurate doesn't matter. The castle molds enhance the imagery and inspire our imaginations.

Once in while, those of us who use sand molds will hear an occasional disparaging word or two from a passer-by, "Oh, sure. It looks pretty good, but that's because they're using those castle molds. That's why it's so good."

It's the sort of commentary we need to completely ignore. We're in the sand, digging, molding, carving and shaping -- with our friends and family. It's our work that has the vast majority of people pausing to smile and offer their "nice job" perspective. We're the people who get to admiringly sit back and enjoy our work with the full knowledge that we did it, together. Remember, the

beautiful framed 8 X 10 photo will hang in our home as a permanent reminder of our artistic creation.

Those of us who spend too much time yearning to be at the beach are constantly searching for new and interesting sand molds. Still, as with golf or carpentry, there are a few basic clubs and tools we should have in our bag.

For sand castles there are a few essential plastic molds we should have in our mesh beach bag or canvas sand-tool bag:

- A single cone-top tower
- A round tower with protective blocks
- A rectangular wall with protective blocks
- A castle corner wall with cone-top tower
- A castle corner wall with a flat-roof upper level and protective blocks

These essentials are in any beach shop. Flimsy molds should be avoided. Smooth sturdy plastic is ideal and used by manufacturers, such as Artoy®, American Plastic Toys®, Come-Play®, Processed Plastics®, Amloid®, Toysmith® and Beachworks®. Beachworks has an especially interesting series of sand castle tools to create stone walls, passageways, stairs and other realistic details and textures.

Different people. Different tools. Unique castles. No two are ever the same because of the zillions of potential variations in the mix of people, tools, beaches, sand, weather and our mood this morning.

Carving Details Into the Sand

Once we really grasp the feel of carving and cutting sand, we can shop for "sand cutlery" tools online, through mail-order catalogs or at specialty shops. One example is a seven-piece set of specialty tools from Sons of the Beach© Designs. These tools are used to carve particular shapes into sand -- columns, the indentations for pillars, squared corners and doorways, narrow windows and virtually any cut into the sand that's imaginable.

Many veteran sand sculptors view the flat stick as the preeminent, universal sand sculpting beach tool. As mentioned earlier, it can be from a broken fence slat, but there are any number of alternative variations off of the flat-stick concept. A simple foot-long length of 1 X 2 smooth lattice strip is probably in the basement waiting for a trip to the beach. Perhaps there's an old wooden ruler in the desk drawer. Or, noting the architectural structures of the book, SAND-tiquity©, a sand sculptor designed a unique flat stick with a rib-like handle on one side. Regardless of its origin, the flat stick is an essential tool for those who play in the sand.

Carving cutlery for sand is available on line. These particular stainless steel sand scalpels are a product of Texas' Sons of the Beach.

The fabulously functional toy shovel can range in length from five to 10 inches. Any larger and it becomes unwieldy and may result in accidental damage to sand structures. Any smaller and it'll certainly disappear -- lost in the sand. After working with the artistic medium of sand and experimenting with a variety of sand tools and molds, consider the useful functionality of the simple toy shovel:

- **Shovels small amounts of sand into small gaps and holes.**
- **Digs small holes.**
- **Carves straight down into the sand to create a nearly vertical wall.**

Smooths flat or slightly rounded sand by gently tapping and pressing with the flat surface of the little shovel face.

Creates a structure's windows, doors, gun slits, protective blocks, stairways, roadways, pathways and moats -- almost anything we'd like to be about 1-2 inches wide or high -- by gently tapping into the structure with the shovel handle.

Want a sly smile on a sculpted sandy face? Press the shovel straight where the mouth should be. In the end, there are dozens or great sand tools for novices and pros. But all it takes for anyone to make memories of a day at the beach are a pail, a flat stick and a small plastic shovel.

The small plastic sand shovel is the singularly most underrated yet artistically versatile sand instrument in our tool box.

Basic tools are all we need to build some really great sand sculptures. Start with a decent two-foot high pile of sand and use a toy plastic shovel and a flat stick -- about the size of wood paint stirrer -- to carve away at the pile.

Cup Castle. Plastic sand castle molds provide exquisite details to an otherwise lumpy pile of sand. But if we find ourselves without plastic molds, just look to our trash for plastic and paper cups and shapes of any kinds. Almost anything can serve as an artistic tool with the forgiving medium of sand.

VI. ABSOLUTELY ANYONE CAN BUILD GREAT SAND CASTLES

A *Day at the Beach* is a book with a mission. That mission is to encourage the creation of great beach memories and demonstrate the pure personal pleasure that comes through sand castle construction.

The two -- nice memories and nice sand castles -- can be effectively linked to one another, thereby improving everyone's overall beach experience.

Superb sand castles are truly magnificent to see. They are towering and majestic. They dominate a section of the beach, demand attention and encourage awe. Vacationers stop to pose for photos. Passersby point. Couples stand near, whisper and smile. Parents protect the castles by restraining little children tugging to plunge into the artistic rendering.

Within this environment, castle builders nod their thanks to scores of people who eagerly toss out praise and admiration. In this beach gallery, sand sculptors smile and quietly offer rudimentary explanations about sand carving and factors such as sand moisture. But by and large, there is rare encouragement that we should take the time and effort to build a sand castle. It seems as though there is too little encouragement for us to participate in what we are praising.

Once in a while on this stage of sand, castle builders take some time to share the craft of sand castle building with others. Those who teach, may use this as a classroom textbook, but the beach, itself, is the lab experience.

A 30-inch pile of water dampened sand can provide about four hours of castle-sculpting play for one person.

Fact is, beach sand is an extraordinarily forgiving and easy art medium with which to work.

From a pile of sand to a molded sand castle can be enjoyed and accomplished by any number of people -- from a couple to half a dozen. This is a 30-inch pile. A larger 4-foot pile of sand allows for larger group participation, especially once work begins to spread away from the top of the pile.

GREAT ROLES IN SAND SCULPTING: THE DIGGER.

WE NEED A PILE OF SAND AS A STARTING POINT FOR OUR SAND CASTLE OR SAND SCULPTING. SO, WE NEED DIGGERS WHO CAN HANDLE A SHOVEL. WE CAN TAKE TURNS WITH ONE SHOVEL, OR WE CAN KEEP A COUPLE OF THEM GOING, SO LONG AS WE ALTERNATE SAND TOSSING AND DON'T SMACK ONE ANOTHER. ANOTHER SAFER OPTION IS TO SUPPLEMENT SHOVELING WITH BUCKETS AND PAILS TO SCOOP SAND AND INCREASE THE SIZE OF OUR PRE-CONSTRUCTION SAND SITE. THE BIGGER THE PILE, THE MORE DRAMATIC THE FINAL RESULT WILL BE.

Holes in the Sand. Big Piles of Sand.

Drum roll. More drum roll. There are two tricks of the trade. Big building drum roll. Here they are: The "secrets" to sand castle success are digging a pretty big hole and mounding up the sand we removed from the hole.

That's it: Dig a Hole. Make a Pile. These, ladeze and gennelmen, are the major elements of beach play that results in creating great sand castles and warm memories we'll all share with people around us.

"Drizzle castles" are made by channeling watery sand through our hands and fingers onto a spot atop of a sand pile or even on flat sand, to create a type of sand stalagmite. It's a gothic or mystical sort of look that can be done for hours, as long as water is near by.

To expand on the basic concept, here are a few related interpretations for great sand play:

- Dig a big hole that displaces sand.

- Dig a hole and put all the sand from the hole into one pile, rather than around the outside of the hole.

- Use the sand pile to build a castle, fort, monster or mountain.

- The hole need not be round. It can be a crescent that will eventually become a castle moat or lake.

- The bigger the pile of sand, the better the sculpting.

- The bigger the pile of sand, the more people who can be involved and share in the experience.

- Tools for sand sculpting can be almost anything.

With the hole and pile of sand in place, acceptable and workable tools can be as basic as a flat stick, as commonplace as plastic sand toys and as technical as a customized set of sculpting tools. Regardless of what we choose to use, we can create a work of art.

The water's edge varies with the rise and fall of the ocean tides. Best sand building is at the very farthest reach of high tide as it rolls up on the sand.

Building at the high-tide line provides moist sand for our base sand pile and generally assures the building crew that waves probably won't crash into the castles gates any sooner than the projected time of the next high tide.

The Sand Pile

A big pile of sand can last all week, if it's above the high-tide line (see page 31). It can begin as a sand pile, be carved into a castle, morphed into a fort, cut into a spiral-trenched mound for ball rolling, flattened to become a turtle and reshaped into a mermaid. Our uses for a big pile of sand are limitless.

Considering the longevity of a pile of sand, there is value is having a standard garden shovel available as a primary beach tool. It's a tool adults can use to make fast work of sand-pile building, so youngsters can enjoy it quicker. An alternative to a digging with a garden shovel is scooping with buckets and large molds.

Take a break. Once work is underway with a sand castle, we can always take breaks for food, reading and other essential activities without losing our work site. The completed work will be dry and shouldn't be re-worked or touches, but the remaining sand pile awaits the sculptor's return.

GREAT ROLES IN SAND SCULPTING: THE WATER BEARER.

OUR BEST SCULPTING IS POSSIBLE WITH A LARGE MOIST SAND PILE. AN EAGER WATER BEARER CAN CONTINUOUSLY POUR WATER ON TO A SAND PILE AS DIGGERS SHOVEL ON MORE AND MORE SAND. CAREFUL TO AVOID COLLISIONS!

Younger Water Bearers oftentimes will need precise instructions as to where the water can best serve a castle construction site.

Ocean spray and brief rains can preserve, enhance and destroy castle construction, but the end result is always unique.

The Scale of Sand Sculpting

Most sand castles are built in a size and scale that's compatible with plastic sand molds. If there are "people" who reside in our castles, they are probably no taller than a thimble. In fact, we don't populate these standard-sized castles with play people, because they may be lost forever under the first of our crumbling sand walls.

Still, we don't need to limit ourselves to a Medieval scale or to castles. Especially among younger kids, a larger scale many perform better for us. We can build forts, houses, walls, bridges and scenes that befit our glamour dolls, action figures or both. We can create a homogeneous setting of surf-side sand structures, where models and soldiers can relax together in a scale sized uniquely for them. The sand allow us some interesting creative play.

Larger scale and proportions -- as with action figures or similarly sized dolls -- provide a completely different sand construction look from we would normally see at the beach. The larger scale also can be helpful when beach sand is coarse, grainy or not well-suited for small detailed carving.

In a further departure from the dimensions of dolls, action figures and castles, we can also build according to the scale of our trucks, cars or boats. We can construct roadways, walls, docks, loading facilities, villages, streets and any number of sets that fit the scale of our imaginary people and their forms of transportation.

Trucks, boats and cars can give us a scale and proportionality within to work in the sand. By building to the toys' dimensions and environment, we shape buildings and structures than differ from our typical sand play. Instead of castle turrets, we build repair shops. Instead of draw bridges, we construct freeways. It's an entirely different and creative mindset.

Themes in Sand Sculpting

The beauty of the large pile of sand we've accumulated is that we can use it to make whatever we want to make. Our scale can be life-sized and kid-sized. In our sand, we can create matching lounge chairs, a love seat or a car with sand pedals and a beach-bucket steering wheel. We can create a boat, a bathtub or a beach chair.

Or we can go in a totally different direction and sculpt animals and people. Our mound of sand can be a sea turtle, a sea serpent, a mermaid, a grouper or maybe a sunbathing beauty.

Sports? We can shape a football stadium or a NASCAR race track. We can smooth out a baseball field or a bowling alley. We can wet the sand and build a swimming pool.

Whatever our imagination wants to try, we can fashion it from sand.

Bodily exaggerations -- long legs, extra arms, partial burying and other more risqué moldings -- are a diversion from sand castle construction and are much quicker to complete and enjoy. These usually require at least one very patient participant who can be an on-going element of the part-human artwork.

GREAT ROLES IN SAND SCULPTING: THE SCULPTOR.

AS THE ELITE OF SAND PLAY, WE CAN SHAPE THE FLOWING HAIR OF A MERMAID, CUT A WINDING STAIRWAY AROUND A TOWER OR GENTLY TAP IN THE MORTAR LINES OF A BLOCK WALL. ALL WE NEED IS A FLAT-EDGED TOOL.

A castle is complete only when we say it's complete, so its construction process provides us with pleasure as long as we want it to. Adding to our own entertainment, we can blend any number of architectural styles together, depending on the inclination of our participants. Our only design limitations are time and number of available artisans. We can construct for hundreds of feet during the course of several days.

Sand Castles

There's an enduring allure to sand castles structures. No matter whatever else we may carve, we seem to gravitate back to sand castles.

Plastic molds provide us with an excellent start on castle construction, and the scale provided by the plastic molds enable us to convert three-foot piles of sand into structures that appear to be massive, towering Medieval castles full of imaginary knights and damsels.

We enjoy the castle motif, but perhaps most important is the potential for individualized involvement and personal contributions in building sand castles. We can play independent of one another, or we can involve a dozen people in castle construction and carving.

With four people working on four sides of a pile of sand, we can construct a castle that is unique to our day at the beach. No quadrant of the castle will be the same. No tower or turret will be exactly like another's. Each of us can portray our part of the castle as we want to portray it.

With just a couple of plastic molds and toy shovels, we can arrive at any variation in castle style, size and scope. We can build a hundred absolutely excellent castles and no two of them will be the same.

Castle turret rooflines and other cone-like structure can be gently shaped with a flat wood stick. First work around and around a central point, slowly but steadily cutting downward and pushing away more sand.

A finished castle turret or cone structure. After cutting away the vertical sides of a turret or wall, return to the roofline to perfect the conical shape by slightly more carving with the edge of the wood stick. If the roof is already dry, gentle downward patting will work better than carving.

Work downward. Start with a tall pile of sand, work downward and around toward eventually reaching the base of the sand pile. Avoid returning to or reaching over a completed area.

Vertical walls are great crowd pleasers and very much possible among sand structures if the sand is wet enough. Best bet is to soak the pile of sand with each several inches of sand that's added.

Extend tower bases downward. To create very tall castle towers, gently carve downward from where the base of the tower mold ends and perpetuate the tower's vertical line into the untouched sand below the mold.

Maybe there's another feature we enjoy about castle building: It's finished when we say it's finished. Or it's never quite finished and we can add to it forever.

With a sea creature or animal, there's an already accepted image or visualization that we expect to see in the finished sand artwork. We work until that visualization is apparent, and then we're finished. Only then can we sit back and savor our accomplishments.

Scrape downward to shave away sand into near-90-degree vertical walls. Best tools for this are straight edged like a plastic shovel, spatula, flat stick or sand carving blade. Shaving away small amounts of sand with each cut creates uniformity of surface and is less likely to cause a sand collapse.

Smooth upward to compress the sand surface and create a finished appearance. This is a reverse move of scraping downward, using the same smooth-faced tool to gently press the sand into a smooth uniform surface.

Press to flatten the surface of a wall or roof line. A flat smooth-faced shovel, stick or spatula can be used to add precision to a wide flat area of sand. With practice the same gentle pressing can be used to create rounded surfaces. Just an FYI: concave surfaces are nearly impossible to create with flat tools.

Indentations can be gently pressed to the sand castle or building to create windows and doors, weapon slits and roofline features. This same process can be repetitiously carried out to create a bricks-and-mortar look to walls. Best tools are narrow flat-edged items like wood sticks and plastic rulers.

GREAT ROLES IN SAND SCULPTING: THE WALL MASON.

EVERY PROJECT NEEDS WALLS. TO CREATE SHORT, SQUATTY, SHARPED-EDGED OR TOWERING WALLS, THE WALL MASON CAN CALL UPON TOOLS RANGING FROM PLASTIC MOLDS TO SURGICAL CARVING INSTRUMENTS.

Windows and doors provide finalizing details that radically improve a sand structure's appearance and fanciful believability. Try a small comparison -- a simple flat-surfaced wall vs. a flat-surfaced wall with slit windows and a tall doorway. Best results in window and doors come with gently pressing into the sand with desired window or door shape -- as with the rectangular handle of a plastic shovel or the end of a flat stick. Also, there are unique sand tools available and designed just for the purpose of pressing doorway and window shapes into sand structures.

Stairways?
Flip back to pages 45 and 53
to see tools and techniques for
building stairways.

A sand castle is never quite finished and construction continues as long as we or others want it to continue. We can erect a couple of towers and walk away. Or we can expand and expand and expand. A simple but towering sand castle may need a city wall around it. Then, as the tide approaches, the castle and walls may require a harbor and docks. The castle, walls and harbor may lead to a need for villages, homes, churches and arenas, which, in turn, need more walls and protective towers. Will it end? Hopefully not.

All of this can be the play of one person for an hour or a day. Or, this can be the play of dozens of people coming in and out of the castle grounds to build, add, modify and refine what has become our own community structure.

With a sand castle, there are no preconceived visual images. No matter what we carve and mold, it will be unique and one of a kind.

So, why do we build sand castles? We build them because we can make them grow and expand. They seem to have a sense of harmony to them.

Different sand castle results emerge from different people, different days and different beaches. If the same people built a dozen sand castles, each would vary from the others because the beach, itself, seems to encourage creative variety.

Available time and space can determine a sand castle's final appearance. One castle can be constructed by one person in a small space in a matter of minutes. Another castle can be constructed over a wide area by a half dozen people during the course of a full day. As sand sculptors, we can decide the amount of available time and space we want involved with a sand castle.

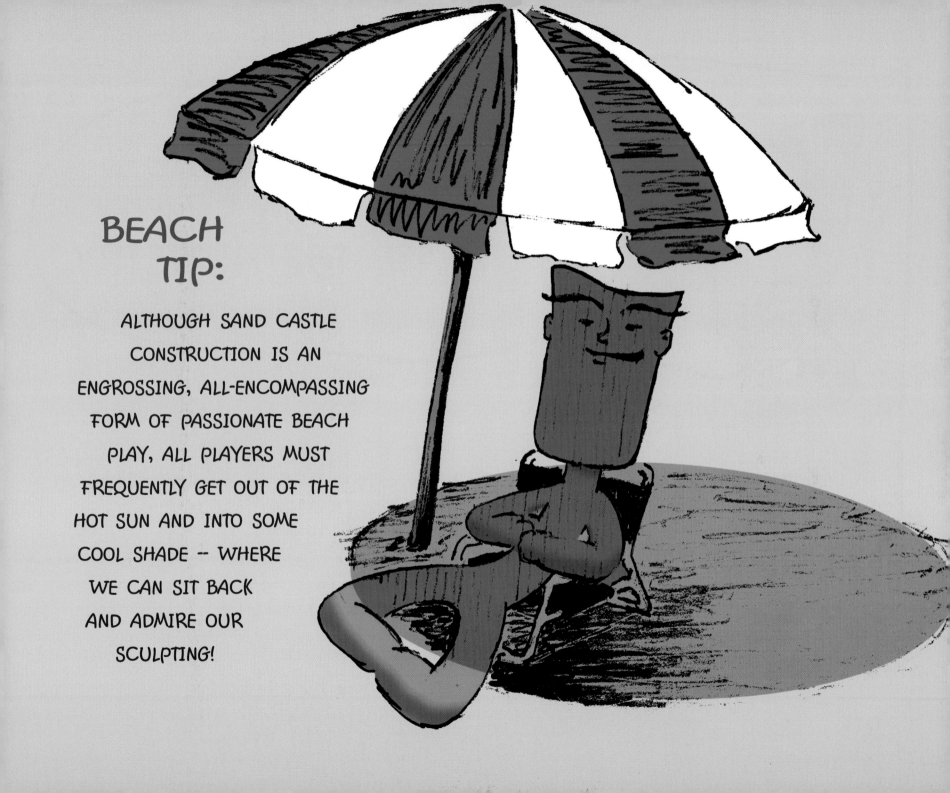

BEACH
TIP:

ALTHOUGH SAND CASTLE
CONSTRUCTION IS AN
ENGROSSING, ALL-ENCOMPASSING
FORM OF PASSIONATE BEACH
PLAY, ALL PLAYERS MUST
FREQUENTLY GET OUT OF THE
HOT SUN AND INTO SOME
COOL SHADE -- WHERE
WE CAN SIT BACK
AND ADMIRE OUR
SCULPTING!

SAND IS JUST THE MEDIUM.
WE CREATE THE ARTISTRY.

It takes only one person can build a sandcastle. It may take an hour. It may take all day. A sand castle or sand sculpture is pretty basic stuff -- mounding up sand, shaping that mound and adding detailed features so the mound imitates reality or conjures up fantasy.

But the greater memories are made when others are involved in the sand construction project and process. Each person will take ownership of a portion of the sand sculpting, and each person will vividly recall the precise tasks and skills accomplished with others. Ten years from now, when we look at that framed photo of our proud clan gathered behind our towering sand castle, each of us will fondly remember our personal interactions that day. Sure, we'll recall the sculpted archway we created, but we'll more vividly recollect the shock we felt and witnessed in each other's eyes when the water caught us from behind, crashed around our ankles and seriously threatened our newly shaped castle courtyard.

VII. GREAT ROLES IN SAND SCULPTING

When we're at the beach and playing in the sand, group involvement is our preference. But with sand castle construction, who does what? Who's makes decisions about size and shape? Who digs? Who builds walls and who builds castle towers? Do participants' ages influence roles we play? What are the skills required to sculpt greatness at the shore?

Honest answer to all of those? Above all, this is play time and relaxed vacation interaction. So, if we've never built a sand castle together, we look to the most experienced sand sculptor for organizational planning and advice. If no one has experience and this is a first-time sand castle, the person holding this book must step forward to offer planning and structure to the process.

Most people would prefer to know our accountabilities in this, our sand castle endeavor. With kids, they just want to know what to do next. Now that one or several of us are in the lead, there are tasks to be assigned to others who have gathered round with their pails, shovels and molds.

In broad terms, the work is fairly labor intensive early on and can become progressively more exacting. That makes sense. We're creating first a pile of sand from a hole in the sand. Later on, that pile gets crafted into something like a Tonka® truck freeway interchange or princess Susan's castle. Thus, the process does somewhat define the jobs.

For those of us who want specific assignments to accomplish before we return to the shade, the blanket and our murder-mystery best seller, then let's consider the potential assignments. A few suggestions are coming right up on the next page.

DIGGER.

Pretty self explanatory. This role is nearly impossible to avoid if we desire a sand castle. We need a pile of sand as a starting point. So, we need diggers who can handle a shovel. We can take turns with one shovel, or we can keep a couple of them going, so long as we alternate sand tossing and don't clobber one another.

SCOOPER.

Akin to the digger, a scooper can work with a bucket to dig and build up our pile of sand. Oftentimes with only one available shovel, the digger and scooper can work on opposite sides of the pile to feed it more and more sand.

WATER BEARER.

Moist sand makes for the best details, whereas dry sand has nearly no adhering properties and will do nothing to fulfill our wishes and a child's dreams of a vertical castle or textured turtle. So, unless we've selected a spot that's about to be overrun by a storm surge, we'll discover that carrying water will be necessary during the early stages of the process. Water bearers are those people who can carry a pail, bucket or some sort of container full of water up from the water's edge to be poured onto our sand pile. The water dumping should be an on-going element of the sand pile preparation.

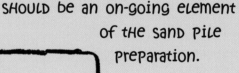

LABORER. Also, pretty self explanatory. This role is extremely key at the beginning of the process and can be a catch-all job title for those tasks already noted. There are times when this role can include errand-running and beverage delivery.

PACKER. One last unskilled labor role is that of the packer, and it's a position that could be formally eliminated, because it's a role that can be easily carried out by one of the other players. As its job title conveys, the packer should pack the sand in the pile. Packers accomplish their task by stomping the pile, slapping it with a shovel or patting their hands hard into the sand. This should take place throughout the digging, scooping and watering process to assure some consistency with the mix of moistness and sturdiness in our sand.

With a small amount of coordination, we can have laborers, diggers, scoopers, packers and water bearers all simultaneously buzzing around our growing mound of sand.

LABORER OR ARTISAN?

As sand construction progresses, the need for artisans overtakes the needs for laborers. With a little practice -- meaning about 10 minutes -- most of us can carry out these more artistic roles, too. Depending on the level of general hand-eye coordination and artistic talent, some of us may demonstrate more precision and skill than others. Some difficulties may arise when smaller kids try tasks they're just not developmentally ready for. In general, there are peripheral tasks that can be gleefully carried out by smaller kids. Beginning on page 92, there is guidance on expectations and age-appropriate levels of beach play.

DIRECTOR OR ARCHITECT. For purposes of beach discussions, we'll consider these two roles as pretty much the same -- the person providing overall visual guidance on our project. If our group is playing on the beach within the metaphor of a stage, then "Director" works. If the sand castle fun is aligned for us as a construction project, then "Architect" is a good term. Basically, this person selects the plot of beach, draws an outline in the sand with his or her heel and proposes our visual direction.

WALL MASON. we will have people among us who become uncomfortable gently shaping sand into what will be the bulging eyes of a frog or a winding staircase around a castle turret. Not everyone has skills in that arena, just as not everyone has skills in law or calculus. Still, we want everyone involved in this. In the case of a sand structure -- castle, house, roadway, fort -- we need walls. Our walls can be short and squatty or tall and narrow. Walls in and around a structure can be smoothly flowing or rigid squares and rectangles with edges and corners. The "look" is what the wall mason determines is best. In the case of a sand sculpted sea animal, it, too, could probably use a protective fence or wall.

SMOOTHER. eventually, all participants in our sand fun will get to carry out all of the roles we outline here. we adapt to the roles where we are most comfortable, and in doing so it's important that we recognize that all tasks do need to be performed. As with a wall mason, a smoother may not be confident with precise sand carving but may easily be able to make sand silky smooth or somewhat textured. It doesn't matter -- using hands or flat tools -- a smoother can become accomplished with both.

SAND SHAPER. use of commercial plastic sand molds is encouraged along with memory molding. sand molds makes great shapes and finite detail if we're careful to use moist but not wet sand. During the construction, we should all attempt to make castle towers and walls with plastic molds, thus carrying out the task of sand shaper. (By the way, a clever trick of the sand-construction trade is to use a castle tower mold to shape a precise castle tower and then extensively elongate the height of the tower by carving downward at a slight angle with a stick or toy shovel. By carving downward from the base of our just-placed sand tower, we create a minor reality but an exaggeration of a much taller tower.)

SCULPTOR. because we're carving in sand and shaping a larger mass into a smaller articulated object, we are all sculptors. we could prefer to think of ourselves as artists, and few would argue that point. But the image of sculptor just seems to fit a little better -- as though we have our wooden mallets and chisels in hand and are tapping at a block of marble. As sculptors in the sand, we play with flat-faced tools and narrow points to create very identifiable details that define the overall image our group wants to convey. As sculptors, we can shape the flowing hair of a mermaid or a winding stairway. we notch the mortar between the blocks, add scales to the mermaid and cut the final arch under a bridge.

THE OFFICIAL OBSERVER. There is a specific role oftentimes overlooked or considered less than meaningful to the sand-shaping process. From among our group, official observer -- and there may be several -- parks a beach chair within immediate line of sight of the work in progress. An official observer's tasks may be difficult or virtually non-existent. We may have passive official observers and active official observers. A passive official observer sits nearby with a good book and occasionally nods a smile of constructive appreciation for the work underway. He or she may choose to do absolutely nothing -- no book, no commentary -- but instead gaze out to sea with only the very rare notice of the sand sculpting activities. On the more animated side of the task list, an active official observer is required to make obligatory unsolicited suggestions for improvements to the sand structure. We can ignore all commentary, but the role of active official observer is much sought after in most beach settings. Regardless of observational role, either can play a key role in the development of memorable vacations.

In the end, if our group is pretty lackadaisical about the formal titles, we can blend in a bit more fun and tie names with tasks, e.g., Alice the Artist, Larry the Laborer, Polly Packer, Wally Wall Mason, Sally the Sculptor, Ollie the Offensive Observer.

The memorable opportunities are endless.

VIII. KIDS, CASTLES AND SAND

We all have different outlooks toward the beach and why we're here. Sure, the sun, sand and water attract us, but what we do in that environment ranges from extreme parasailing to paperback-book-page-turning.

Our interests differ. So we'd be goofy to if we didn't recognize that all kids interact with sand in various ways, depending on their age, sex, level of interest, attention span, general disposition and any number of personal and outside influences. Still, believe it or not, children act fairly predictably at the beach. As adults, we can better understand kids' expectations, improve their beach play and add to their beach memories.

The nitty gritty of acquiring these skills is found in the works of the child development masters like as Swiss biologist and psychologist Jean Piaget, whose theories, concepts and writings continue to influence teaching, even decades after his death. But since beaches are supposed to be about mental relaxation, here's a dumbed-down version -- a basic summary of what we can expect from kids at the beach.

In general, beach play and sand castle building have a positive effect on nurturing children or -- from a parental, grand-parental and neighborly perspective -- merely wanting to enjoy the kids a bit more. The toy industry looks to facilitate improved child growth and greater adult-child interaction. From a practical point of view, such growth and interaction generate toy product sales. From a theoretical point of view, society benefits when children learn patience and improved communications. The toy industry, in general, and the beach toy industry, more precisely, understand their value in promoting creative thinking among children and strengthening kids' ability to acquire new knowledge.

Kids will improvise their creative play to adapt to the sand at hand. Immediate access to water is always an advantage.

Stages of Child Development

Jean Piaget's simple theory of childhood development embraced four stages which can be easily aligned with sand sculpting to predict how kids will behave at the beach and how adults can use the experience to help them grow. Piaget outlined four stages:

- Birth - two years old is the Sensorimotor stage, when a child uses physical interaction to build concepts about reality.

- Ages 2 - 7 is the Preoperational stage, when children need concrete physical situations, because they are not able to understand abstracts.

- Ages 7 - 11 is the Concrete Operations stage, when a child is conceptualizing and creating internal structures to explain his or her own physical experiences. Abstracts are becoming understandable.

- And ages 11 - 15 are the beginning of Formal Operations stage, when children are pretty much adult in their conceptual reasoning.

If it's not too hot, sand is one of the great tactile sensations for infants.

Two and Under

For kids who are two and under, the world is a fireworks display experienced from the inside. There is just so much to take in and absorb. If a day at the beach is a new and unique experience, we can expect they will love it. Still, we should expect nothing in the way of actual constructive play and sculpting from these little guys.

Knowing this age group is rapidly building "mental maps" with each experience, this is where the wonderful memories begin. With sand play, a toddler wants to basically move sand from one spot to another without any idea of why or intended results. Small beach toys -- shovels, pails, shapes and forms, along with some pretty neat funnels and turning wheels -- are available to move soft, dry sand. The same basic ideas will work with water, as long as it's not too cold.

An idea that combines play and corralling is to drag an empty wading pool to the beach and fill it with just the right amount of water from the surf.

Of greatest importance at this stage is that wobbling little kids cannot protect themselves from anything -- sun, heat, cold, water, wind, blowing sand, gulls or anything else that might present itself at our spot in the sand. And let's not pretend, most little kids' inclination with sand is to eat it, at least once.

Sand collapses. The water causes it. Weak foundations cause it. Sometimes it just happens in the midst of our construction. The neat trick is to convert that collapse into an interesting or functional design element.

In this case, we lost the corner of an action figure building because of rising water. Water rolled in and undermined the corner near the doorway. Frustrating as that is, sand remains a very flexible medium for our art. We can re-carve the corner and change the architectural appearance.

Eventually, the water wins. It's only a matter of time with high tide or a storm surge. No matter how many sand barriers we construct, the water will slowly erode the sand and our construction back down to where it is near sea level. So? Tomorrow we can build again.

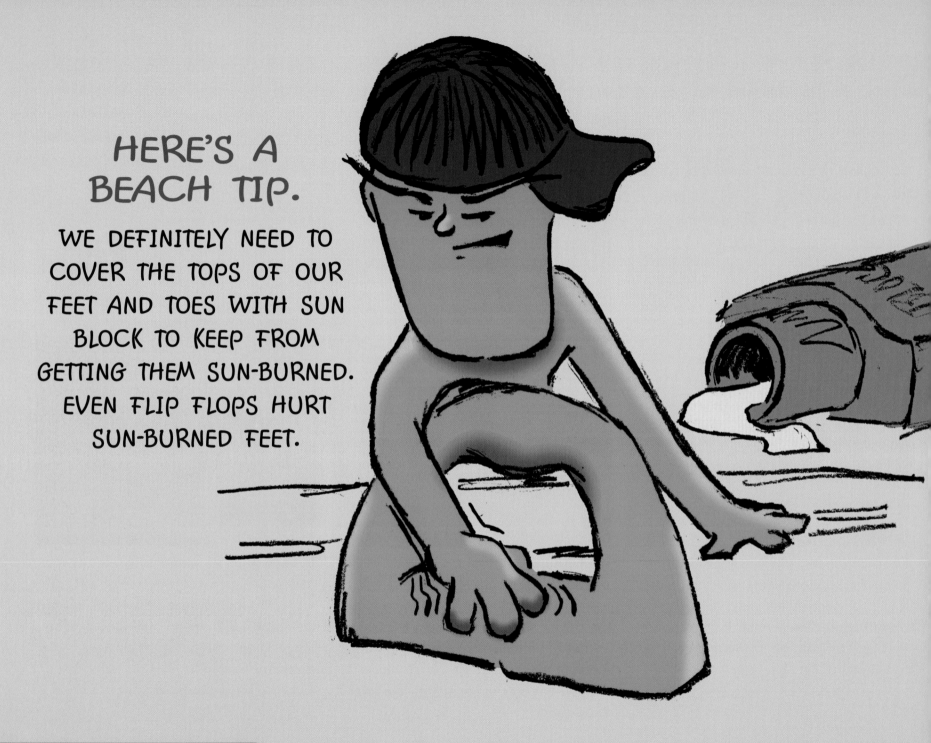

HERE'S A BEACH TIP.

WE DEFINITELY NEED TO COVER THE TOPS OF OUR FEET AND TOES WITH SUN BLOCK TO KEEP FROM GETTING THEM SUN-BURNED. EVEN FLIP FLOPS HURT SUN-BURNED FEET.

Ages Two to Seven

Between the ages of two and seven, kids go through major changes in how they play at the beach. As a result, an annual beach vacation will offer extremely different memories during this five-year span. We'll experience some rapid growth, plus changes in interests and intellectual understanding. As a three year old, our child remains self-focused, unsharing and remaining in one within one physical environment for brief periods. No surprises there.

At three, we're digging, dumping and sifting. These are alluring pastimes for this youngster, as long as all around remains fairly constant and non-distracting. Hole-digging is a satisfying process. We may get some side by side play or some mimicking of older kids, but, again, not much sharing.

Major beach items at this early age are sand pails, sand shovels, funnels and wheels and anything we can use to transport sand from one spot to another. On the other hand, we're less stationary, and we want to push sand around a little more than last year.

Dozens of sand sculpting toys are fantastic and add to beach play, but the basic essentials are a plastic sand shovel and a pail that doubles as a castle tower. Literally, children and adults or any age can find creative uses for these two sand toys.

Children between the ages of three and seven begin to see patterns and systems to life and their surroundings. This might explain how kids identify big piles of sand as having great value for play. From their munchkin perspective, adult-created piles of sand are enormous mountains to climb. Once at the pinnacle, they become heights from which to roll and slide. A sand pile has virtuoso uses for a six year old. It's an auto race track, Jeep proving grounds, army fort and backyard garden. It's a ski resort, sea monster and multi-person vehicle. The monster pile of sand is a monster contributor to beach memories.

At the other end of shovel spectrum is digging holes in the sand. If we haven't noticed, some youngsters move sand and discover they can easily dig a good-sized hole. With some luck and correct water-proximity positioning by parents, the diggers also discover that water appears in the bottom of the hole. Wow. Dig in dry sand, and water sneaks into the bottom. How cool is that?

As sharing begins to occur with a fair amount of regularity, sand play among several kids becomes more enjoyable for everyone with a 20-foot radius. Adults will still need to referee squabbles over who has beach mineral rights or whose turn it is to operate the milling wheel, but at this age, there is a calm now possible at the beach -- something that was less frequent during the first few years of kids' beach play.

The basics of motivational encouragement and positive re-enforcement are important to parenting during this time at the beach,

because each day is a new experience for kids who are each day venturing into new ground. Whether sifting of plowing, now is a time for instruction and praise.

Recall, before the age of seven, children are still focused on concrete and physical situations to which they can easily relate and understand. Abstract problem solving is still a year or so away for most. Perhaps this age of two to seven is when plastic sand molds begin to earn their greatest importance. Whether molds of sea

For kids, the water's edge is where they can be their most energetic and creative with sand and water.

creatures or sea side castles, the plastic molds are several levels of concrete reality. The plastic image of a castle tower can be a toy on to itself. But using that plastic tower to create a nearly identical sand tower is a very satisfying feat. This result is not abstract. It is tangible and real.

Sand structures can match the scale and theme of our toys, whether they're planes, trains or automobiles. In this instance, thinking ahead to bury horizontal sticks in a sand pile allows us to carefully dig under those sticks and create a tunnel or bridge.

Ages Seven to 11

Between Seven and 11, kids see issues as cut and dry, black and white. Their reactions and emotions echo that, so we don't experience many middle ground or gray situations. Toward 11 and 12, abstracts and concepts become more a part of youngsters' lives, but not during the earlier portion of this age period.

This group will likely respond well to some role-playing at the beach -- role-playing as the sand-work tasks described by San D. Shovel in "Great Roles in Sand Sculpting." Briefly, there are assignments and tasks for kids to carry out in working with a sand sculpture. Most seven-year-olds find comfort in everyone else having assigned tasks, especially when the tasks come with everyone also having an assigned title. They'll be superb Diggers and Scoopers, able to prepare the site for sand construction. Seven and eight-year-olds grasp the need for the accountabilities of being Water Bearers or Laborers. And they match up well with tasks as Sand Packers and Wall Masons.

Sand play and modifications offer an opportunity to be creatively flexible.

Although this age group enjoys the tasks and titles, it's an adult or older child judgment call as to when 10-year-olds should be encouraged as Sculptors. A good interim training ground in sand play is with wall-building, during which the older Director can make a determination as to the progress of the younger task-holder.

Recall that these kids are very much learning through hands-on experience. Performing certain skilled sculpting tasks may be in the future for some children but more immediately at hand for others. The key is how we adjust and adapt and how much encouragement the kids feel.

Beach play and sand sculpting are excellent for learning mental and emotional flexibility and adaptation. This age group is very much learning through trial and error with everything they do, including their day at the beach. When it comes to helping this group or teaching the individual kids, sand is a great erasable chalk board.

Picture it. Sand collapse? Repair it in 30 seconds. There's no need for frustration or anger. Sand modifications offer an opportunity to be creatively flexible.

Scale of sand sculpting can be important with kids under 12. They're going to be fascinated with how they can play with a blend of toys and sand. Their trucks, cars, action figures and some dolls seem to be natural and easy with the beach and its environment.

Adults and older kids have an opportunity to further enhance the younger kids' enjoyment by proposing or building forts, walls and buildings that fit the scale of larger toys. Most sand molds are designed for small scale structures, best befitting very young kids who admire a single sand tower or older kids who can relate to the fantasy of European castles. But larger scale can be perfect for an 11-year-old. There's nothing wrong with a good smooth 12-inch

Water in the hole doesn't always spell complete sand castle disaster, but it can be a sign that it's time to sit back and watch the tide fill the moat.

GREAT ROLES IN SAND SCULPTING: THE SAND SHAPER.

PLAYERS IN THIS ROLE HANDLE THE SOMETIMES TRICKY PLASTIC CASTLE MOLDS. THEY MUST PRACTICE NEAR OUR CONSTRUCTION SITE TO GET A GOOD FEEL FOR THE CORRECT SAND-WATER CONSISTENCY TO BE USED IN THE MOLDS.

wall built to protect Work Out Barbie from a meddlesome GI Joe.

During this period in our lives -- seven to 11 -- we're expanding our mental capabilities so that we can have real conversations about sand play techniques and skills and approaches to try. Again from the experts, concepts can become physical realities and abstracts can become real. Castle sculpting is very interesting to observe and more interesting to attempt. It's one of those things that can move from imagination to concrete imagined reality within, literally, just a few minutes.

A sand castle. Imagine it. Create it.

Simply pushing sand with our hands or feet becomes the start of sand sculpting. Children find the best sand. Adults can offer a few tools.

Ages 11 to 15

Are there people out there who didn't experience the wide, wide spectrum of growth, change and emotions that occurs during puberty? We all pass through this portal. The struggle of the passage varies only in degrees of difficulty. So of course, any discussion about beach play in relation to this age group merely touches the very tip of the proverbial iceberg.

Then, there are the 12-year-old castle stompers. This much maligned group is usually boys. They find joy in identifying a nicely built sand castle during the afternoon hours, so they can return at dusk as terrorizing marauders who stomp the detailed castle into grains of sand. It happens. It just happens. Fact is, there are more 12-year-old beach artists and craftspersons than leaping, lunging marauders, but the nasty culprits do perpetuate a surf side reputation that influences society's view of 12-year-old boys.

Hand-shaping of sand can be a starting point to establishing the general theme of a sand castle as it emerges from the large pile of sand.

Child psychologist Jean Piaget theorized that kids in the 11 - 15 age range actually have adult capacity but a wide array of maturity levels. No kidding. what's that mean to me?

Marauding young men also benefit from beach play and sand sculpting. One approach is to encourage circling castle crushers to patiently wait and assist with some castle construction. Two factors can be used to recruit bands of boogy-boarders to work on carving castle walls with small toy shovels: 1) The forthcoming tide is going to get the sand castle anyway before the beach is abandoned for the day and before the boys can launch their attack. 2) Once the structure is complete and before the tide hits, all participating builders can sit back a few feet from the finished sand castle and lob in small beach-stone "bombs" to see how the castle withstands an enemy assault.

The concept encourages patience and participation in the sand sculpting.

Lobbing foam-ball "bombs" at a finished sand castle can be one way to wrap up the day and the enjoy a castle just as the tide begins to roll in to reclaim the sand.

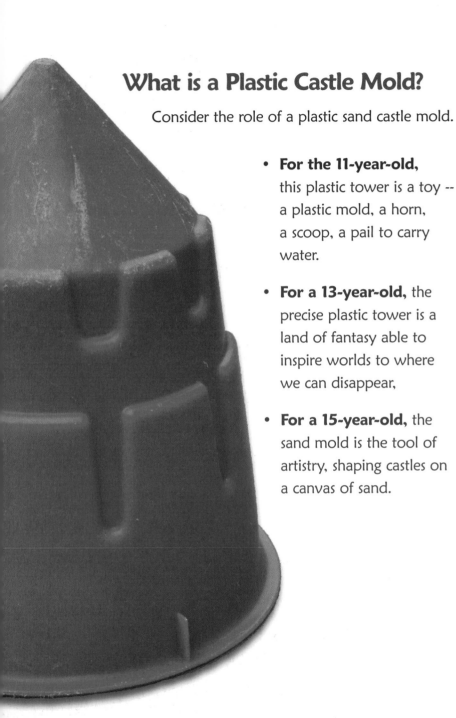

What is a Plastic Castle Mold?

Consider the role of a plastic sand castle mold.

- **For the 11-year-old,** this plastic tower is a toy -- a plastic mold, a horn, a scoop, a pail to carry water.

- **For a 13-year-old,** the precise plastic tower is a land of fantasy able to inspire worlds to where we can disappear,

- **For a 15-year-old,** the sand mold is the tool of artistry, shaping castles on a canvas of sand.

Pre-teen and young teens learn from the beach's tactile experiences. Sand stomping is a visible sign. But we also see kids burying one another in the sand and their rolling in the sand.

Imagination is enabled in a beach setting. There's just something about the sand and the beach that tells us to broaden our experiences and be more accepting of our own whimsical play. Even at 13, we certainly wouldn't lay in mud in our backyard, but we'll dig a water-filled beach hole and lounge back into what we call "the cave man's first hot tub."

Sand successes vary from child to child -- whether it's the stairways to castle towers or burying all but the face of your younger brother.

Sand is versatile and allows us to construct buildings to match the scale and theme of children's toys.

GREAT ROLES IN SAND SCULPTING:

THE SAND SMOOTHER II.

THE ROLE OF SAND SMOOTHER MAY REQUIRE HAND PATTING AND SMOOTHING OR CAREFUL WEILDING OF A FLAT STICK OR SMALL SHOVEL. IT IS AN EXCELLENT POSITION FOR CONFIDENCE BUILDING.

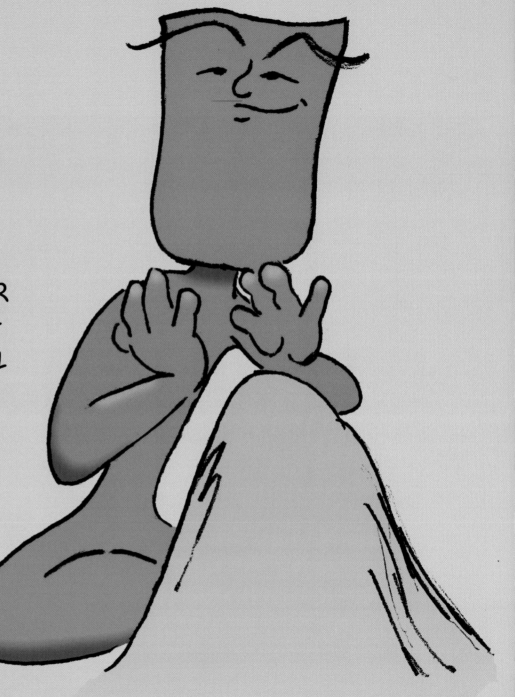

Teens

Teens are at an age where they can accept differing views. The black and white, cut and dry perceptions have given way to intellectual consideration and a capability for objectivity. It now becomes more commonplace for shared learning among teen peers and within a group. Also, according to child development specialists, family and cultural understanding is in place by the age of 14 or 15. Still, while none of this growth means we can immediately overcome the friction that frequently exists between mother and daughter or father and son, these changes do, however, offer us an opportunity for some common ground and partially shared experiences.

If we begin with a decent pile of moist sand -- say three feet high and six feet in diameter -- we have created a circumference of more than 18 feet. If each person wants to have a role in converting our pile into a sand castle, we have coincidently created about six work areas around the pile, each about three feet wide. That means six people can claim a spot and focus on it. This single, big pile of sand can easily accommodate an extended family spanning three generations. Each person elects the design of their narrow work area. Each person can look to others, talk with others but

The crisp carved stairway details come from gently pressing the handle of a small plastic shovel vertically into a smooth ramp of sand to create each individual step. With patience and teaching, most children 10 and older can enjoy the success of building stairways.

only if she or he choose that option. It's also productive to intensely shape a three-foot section of sand immediately and be part of the overall scheme of sand castle construction.

We easily see that decentralized decision-making is especially apparent with group sand play. We can arrive at a generally shared vision and complete it, together, working in close proximity or on opposite sides of the sand pile. Either way, we've set up an environment in which we are together. Perhaps in that setting, conversations about castles become conversations about life.

Sand carving can attract attention and the opposite sex. For the 11-year-old boy, we see the scowling face and hear a distinctive rasping noise as a young girl shows interest in the young boy's sand carving. But for the 15-year-old boy, we can observe shyness, coyness or flirtatiousness as a 15-year girl stops to observe and comment on the grandeur of the boy's work.

Sand castles, sand carving and sand play can be vehicles to invite close interaction among family, among friends and among strangers.

The Toy Sand Shovel with Children of Different Ages

Despite numerous reports to the contrary, the plastic, toy sand shovel is, indeed, many things to many people. Among children, the shovel can play at least a dozen roles. Consider:

Ages 1 - 2	The toy sand shovel is used for tossing sand in the air.
Ages 2 - 3	The shovel can move sand from one site to another site a few inches away.
Ages 4 - 5	It's a cartoon character.
Ages 4 - 7	The shovel is a shovel for digging small holes in wet sand.
Ages 5 - 10	The shovel can load small trucks. It's a road construction vehicle. It's a roadway paver and smoother. It's a sand sled for small toy soldiers.
Ages 7 - 11	Shovels join together to become play characters with others of multi-colored shovel persuasions.
Ages 8 - 12	The sand shovel becomes a weapon or tool for action figures.
Ages 10 - 12	It doubles as radar antenna in a fort.
Ages 12 - 14	The shovel returns to its roots to create the walls of a castle moat.
Ages 13 - adult	A sand shovel is used as a carving, smoothing and notching tool in creating sand structures.
Ages 14 - adult	The plastic toy sand shovel takes on the persona of a sand sculpting scalpel.

GREAT SAND SCULPTING ROLES FOR KIDS.

Ages 11 into teens -- TALENT AND SKILLS ARE PLENTIFUL. AT THESE AGES, KIDS SHOULD GIVE A TRY TO ALL SAND SCULPTING TOOLS AND TECHNIQUES: TALL TOWERS, STAIRWAYS, OVERHANGING ROOFLINES, ETC.

Ages 7-11 -- PLASTIC CASTLE MOLDS CAN BE NICELY MASTERED TO CREATE LONG SECTIONS OF CASTLE WALLS AND TURRETS. LARGER VERSIONS OF DOORS, WINDOWS AND STAIRS ARE VERY POSSIBLE AND LIKELY SUCCESSFUL.

Ages 2-7 -- MOSTLY GROUND-LEVEL WORK, USING STRAIGHT-EDGED TOOLS TO CONSTRUCT RAMPS, ROADS, DRAW BRIDGES, TUNNELS, MOUNDS AND WALLS.

Infant - 2 -- SAND PLAY IS MOVING IT FROM ONE SPOT TO ANOTHER THROUGH SIFTERS, WHEELS, FUNNELS, PAILS AND CONTAINER OBJECTS.

ADULTS, CASTLES AND SAND

Working adults vacationing at a beach view sand sculpting somewhat differently than younger beach patrons. As a total shift away
from the rigors of work or careers, adults find sand to mesmer-
izing, absorbing, relaxing and satisfying. Sand play can offer an
intense focus complimented by the success of completing a project.
Just another day at the beach.

BEACH TIP:

LET'S MAKE SURE WE HAVE PLENTY OF WATER OR DRINKS NEAR BY. SAND CRAFTING CAN BE VERY STRENUOUS ON A HOT BEACH.

IX. SUNSETS AND SAND

At some point at the end of the day, we need to quit playing in the sand. At some point, wind, rain or tides will flatten any sand structure, including the finest of sand castles. Some structures will last a few days, but eventually they will return to join all other sand.

There's not much we can do about this natural occurrence. Instead, we play with it. We live with it. We build at a spot where the tide will reach our harbor and topple our castle towers. Only then can we experience the full sand castle cycle:

From nothing, to a pile to sculpted art. From sculpted art holding off the tide to a pile of sand to nothing. It's a magnificent process to share.

A DAY AT THE BEACH:

A BOOK FOR CREATIVE FUN AND HELPFUL INFORMATION FROM **EDUCATIONAL BEACH PRESS**

In a fully pleasant world, we'd want to be only where we are happiest. Because that's not possible, Educational Beach Press hopes to help people create satisfying days, savor their moments, gather enjoyable memories and draw strength and happiness from those days when the world is less than a fully pleasant place to be.

Educational Beach Press emerged through Doug Smith, its founder and Chief Creative Officer. He authored *A Day at the Beach* and provided illustration, photography and design. Other beach-related works are available through www.EducationalBeachPress.com.

PHOTOGRAPHIC CREDIT

Beyond photography by Doug and Sue Smith, additional work for A Day at the Beach came from friends and family:

Scott Smith, pages 6, 28, 70, 99, 103, 113.

Harry Dunlavy, pages 9, 19, 26, 27, 40, 61, 114, 118.

John and Sara McIntyre, pages 14, 32, 56, 79.

Angie and Jim Moore, pages 19, 36, 92.

Ron and Joanne Baumgartel, 19, 23, 30, 36, 37, 39, 42, 43.

Kevin and Peggy Hoag, pages 21, 68.

Bridgid and George Grode, page 29

Tanya Delellis, pages 31, 96.

Donald VanKirk, pages 47, 48, 50, 62, 79, 102.

From the most seasoned professional photographer of the bunch, Sue's dad, the late Richard W. Hoag, 1918-2002, pages 78, 80, 103 and 111.

ACKNOWLEDGEMENTS by D.R. Smith

This is my public thank you to the genuine and caring people who contributed to this book. The list of those who supported the concept of A Day at the Beach is amazingly long and cannot be completely included. Maybe that's because so many friends and family have been involved in creating the real better beach memories woven in among these pages.

Still, I need to mention a few people. In addition to Sue and my boys and sculpting companions, Scott and Todd Smith, the book's guiding tone comes from Angie, Jim and toddler Mallory Mae Moore. Thanks to Nathan Sargent for his challenge to write; and thanks to my most frequent and fun castle-carving friend and brother-in-law, John McIntyre; his wife, my sister Sara; their daughters Kelsey and Jamie; and my entrepreneurial in-laws

who provided not only encouragement but facts, photos and direction, Kevin and Peggy Hoag, along with Cassie and Abby. My near-family acknowledgments must go to the closest thing I have to a brother who doubles as book-editor-supreme and his wife and our friends, Bill and

Pam Drellow; overall editorial and creative support from Terry and Tresa Seaford; editing and encouragement by Karen Early; and emotional support from my post-employment support group of Steve and Kim Sanker. Professionally, Dave Clark of Right Management and

author Douglas Lee Gibbony consistently said press on. Then, at my side throughout this with design, critiques and creativity was Tom Kolarich.

Even on the best of days, a beach isn't always near by for play or for book preparation. Sometimes a suburban sidewalk has to double as a beach photography set.